Understanding Behaviour

*Psychology for parents, and teachers
working with family groups*

2

Madan Mall

Berni Stringer

The Questions Publishing Company Ltd
2002

The Questions Publishing Company Ltd
Leonard House, 321 Bradford Street, Digbeth, Birmingham B5 6ET

First published in 2002

ISBN: 1-84190-054-0

Illustration and design: Al Stewart
                            John Minett
Editorial team: Amanda Greenley
                            Linda Evans

Printed in the UK

Contents

Part one: You and your childhood

Part two: Being a parent

Part three: Bonding and attachment

Part four: Communicating with each other

Part five: Families . . . and living in them

Part six: Learning from experiences

Dedications and author biographies

Madan Mall

My special thanks to Baba Hardev Ji for his support and continuous guidance.

To John Burnham and David Lake for having the greatest influence in my systemic thinking. Barry Pope for Cognitive Behaviour Therapy and Personal Construct Psychotherapy. My colleagues at SSD: Child and Adolescent Mental Health Service with whom I have enjoyed my 12 years of working life.

To Mike Clarke and Charlie Mead for their encouragement and advice.

To my family, especially my brother Gurcharan Mall who is always making me laugh.

Most of all thank you to the children and the families with whom I have worked.

Madan Mall is an experienced child and family therapist and is presently working with EVITA training in Birmingham providing specialist provision for children, aged 10–17, with emotional behavioural difficulties.

Madan has had 22 years' experience working with children and families in a variety of agencies in the West Midlands. He is an associate lecturer with The Open University, and is currently undertaking a doctorate in Counselling Psychology. He is the proud father of three teenage children.

Berni Stringer

For Michelle and my mom and dad – gone too soon. For Keith, Chris and Josie who have cooked their own tea many times, much love.

Thank you for my experience of families.

I wish to acknowledge the strengths of the many children who have allowed me into their lives to witness their fortitude.

Thank you for all you have taught me about children.

Berni Stringer is a qualified teacher and social worker with an advanced qualification in supervision and mentorship in childcare from the University of Leicester. She is presently working as a senior practitioner in a local authority Camhs, offering a service primarily to children in public care, foster carers and families.

She has a long-standing interest and concern for children's mental health and has worked in residential, education and local authority settings using cognitive behavioural methods and direct play work. She has a particular interest in attachment issues. Berni is also a part-time Dip SW tutor and lecturer in work with children and families.

Introduction

This book has been written as a result of the authors' extensive involvement with children and those who care for and educate them. The authors have had a combined total of over 35 years' experience.

Together we have shared the experiences of many children and listened to their stories. Here you will find the concentrated wisdom of many researchers, psychologists and childcare experts whose ideas and concepts have been influential in our work, and that of other childcare practitioners in the past.

This book is written for parents, carers and others who have daily contact with children who are troubled by the challenges that face many families. We have worked with many caring and committed adults who strive to support children and help them to reach their potential. We have included many of the exercises and conversations that we, and those we have worked with, have found helpful in the past. For the most part, this book is constructed as if it were a conversation with a parent or carer, and is aimed at those who wish to try resolving their concerns before they seek external help.

Bringing up children is quite probably the most challenging task you will ever undertake.

The training is minimal, and designed only to cover the starter pack – the bottles, nappies and the rash – during the first three months of feeding, nappy changing and sleepless nights. There is no top-up training, only skills developed with on-the-job experience.

The financial recompense is negligible and eaten up (literally!) in overheads and accompanying hardware, and gets more costly over time. Resources and person power are limited and you don't get days off for sick leave or holidays. For many it is one of two full-time jobs. It can be a lonely and isolating job, and one that does not really leave you free to choose to work elsewhere.

It can feel as though everyone else is an expert, having been there and done that, except *you*.

And you can never top someone else's birth, tantrum or sleepless night stories.

So why do people do it?

Why do people let themselves in for the longest and most challenging task of their lives?

Is it, as some would believe, a primal urge to procreate, or is it an incredibly selfish desire to extend facets of oneself into the future? Perhaps caring for children is the most fantastically generous gesture that one can make to society, one's partner, oneself…or one's family!

Most people would agree that child-rearing is an intensely personal experience that is, for the most part, challenging and fulfilling for the majority of parents and carers. However, childcare is essentially a private activity that occurs behind closed doors – except of course for the tantrums at the checkout.

When it is going well, people do the task without thinking, live the joys and relish the contentment. The satisfaction is enormous and the feedback ("mummy I love you" or "what beautiful children") is heart-stopping. Your confidence as an able and capable carer, who can love and be loved, grows daily. You can experience extremes of emotion not given to you by any other experiences. And you can revisit childhood experiences that you enjoyed or missed the first time round.

But what about when it is going badly?

There are times when you truly feel that you have lost the plot, or that you and your child are not playing by the same rules (or even the same game). For example, when your child reaches some new stage of development or a phase that you just don't believe will pass, or when your anxieties escalate because your child challenges you with behaviour that you are positive will lead to anti-social tendencies in the future.

As caring and responsible parents/carers you will try to work out what has gone wrong and rectify it. If that doesn't work you may well look for advice from family and friends and, finally, from the professionals. At this point your child-rearing practices become a public activity, and your experiences are open to scrutiny and expert opinion.

Ask the experts

Experts are people who are knowledgeable about children's development, health, learning and behaviour. They may be teachers, health visitors, doctors, social workers or psychologists, or well-meaning family members. When you are struggling, or think you've got it all horribly wrong, you are convinced they know what is best for your children better than you do.

So what do they do?

Professionals are there to help. The theoretical school of thought that a professional adheres to will determine the advice or help you get for a concern you have.

For example, a psychologist using a behavioural approach will view behaviour as learnt and reinforced by positive experiences. You may then be advised about rewards, boundaries and time-outs and might well come away from the consultation clutching a star chart to tackle a wet bed.

If, however, the professional is of a psychoanalytical orientation, you may well be encouraged to explore your relationship with your child and look for any inherent anxieties, including their relationship with you, which may underlie the bed-wetting. With the insight you gain you will be enabled to resolve the problem, particularly if you have explored it through your relationship with your therapist.

Perhaps your professional is a medical person, for example a doctor. In this case you are likely to leave the consultation with a prescription for medication or a buzzer and pad.

If you happen to mention your concern to a social worker, you could end up applying for a grant for new laundry. A teacher would look for signs of bullying, a health visitor for signs of rivalry with a new sibling. If you mention your worry to your great aunt, she may say your child is over indulged. Or your neighbour with six well-behaved children may tell you that your 'problem child' will 'grow out of it'.

Of course these are all stereotypical examples (and somewhat tongue in cheek!), but the point is that everyone can seem to be an expert except you.

So, what is the point of all this?

The point is that 'the professionals' view the problem from the perspective, and from within the learning, that they have found helpful in the past. In many cases external help and advice is imperative – it can resolve difficulties and retrieve family relationships.

However, we believe that **you** are the expert on your child.

How to use this book

This book is written primarily for use by, or with, parents and carers of children and aims to help you tackle your concerns early, in creative and loving ways that suit the needs of yourself and your child. We believe that, although prevention is better than cure, ongoing relationship-building between adults and children is imperative, and if a problem does arise there *are* steps you can take to deal with it yourself. If you then seek further advice, you will have helpful information to assist 'the professional' in assessing and supporting you as you resolve the problem.

In the first sections of this book, the exercises are designed to help you think about the ideas you already have concerning how children should behave. However, if problems have already arisen then working through these exercises will at least stop them getting worse, and may even help to improve the situation.

You will find references to theory, questions, activities, thinking tasks and discussion points. The examples included are designed to help you work out what you know from your own experience of being a child, and from caring for your children so far. If, eventually, you make a decision to seek external help, you will find that you have already done much of the groundwork that will help the professional to help you.

If you are working through the book by yourself, and you choose to complete the exercises, you will find it useful to keep a notepad and pencil because, as you work through, you will have the opportunity to reflect on your knowledge and experience, and begin to develop plans for the future. Keep the notes that you make. When you have finished you will have a journal to pass to your children.

You may find it helpful to ask someone to discuss some of the issues with you – to act as your mentor if you like – and to notice and comment on changes or differences.

You may decide to work through this book with a partner, or someone who shares the responsibility of rearing your child with you. When you have finished reading this book together you will have a shared understanding of how your early experiences have formed your current relationships and how they influence them.

Who might find this book useful?

You will find this book useful if you are a teacher or support worker in a school or unit, a health visitor or social worker, or if you are a practitioner who supports children and families in either statutory or voluntary organisations. This book can be used with individuals, couples or groups and is not just for mothers!

If you are using this book to facilitate a group you will wish to refer to the Bibliography for further reading. We have not divided the book into group sessions, because you will work through all or parts of the book at a pace that suits your group.

We acknowledge that we may not have done justice to the value of the theories we have referenced by not exploring each in depth. This is not the purpose of this workbook. To explore interesting areas further please refer to the reading list at the back of the book.

We are experienced practitioners and trainers in childcare and education. We have used the principles and theories included in this book to inform our practice, and have found practical and accessible ways for you to use them. The purpose of this book is to assist you, as a parent or carer, to apply the thoughts of knowledgeable and experienced researchers and practitioners, whose insight and knowledge has been of assistance to us in our own work, to your own situation.

So, let's begin!

Part one

You and your childhood

You and your childhood

This book will help you to become your own expert in managing your children, sorting out difficulties and spotting problems. Throughout the book you will be asked to undertake various tasks as you work towards solving the problem in hand or prepare to deal with what might come. We believe that you already know the solution to the problem, or at least know what it takes to sort it out.

As with most subjects you probably do not realise how much you know until someone helps you retrace what you have forgotten.

Images

What *images* of children do you see regularly in the media?

Fill in the spaces below with words or images.

Newspapers	Magazines/catalogues

Television	Films

- Are your images mostly good ones?

- What might have influenced your thoughts and images?

- Do you think society generally values its children?

- Consider your reaction when you see images of children in the media who are:
    - abandoned,
    - disabled,
    - poor,
    - abused, or
    - delinquent.

- Do the images you hold change with the circumstances of the child?

Discuss

Discuss with a friend

● What conclusions have you come to about your views and attitudes to children?

● Have your opinions changed with the experience of having your own children?

● If you share your childcare with a partner, are your partner's views similar to your own?

● How will the care of your children be affected if your views differ?

● Would you say your thoughts and ideas about children and their rights are the same or different to those held by your parents?

● Would you hold the same values if you were caring for someone else's children?

● How does the experience of being a child today, compare with your own experiences?

Thinking about these questions will have helped you to consider your own experiences of childhood and bringing up children. You will also have begun to explore the attitudes and images that you and others hold of children. You will have questioned how wider society influences your management of and relationship with children in your care.

How children learn

Knowing how children learn and are influenced can be a useful way of understanding their behaviour. How children learn about appropriate and inappropriate behaviour, good manners, and what is expected of them in certain situations is called *socialisation**.

Hetherington and Parkes (1993) describe socialisation as "the process whereby an individual's standards, skills, motives, attitudes and behaviour are influenced to conform to those regarded as desirable and appropriate for his or her present or future role in society".

In 1975, a study was carried out by John Whiting called the 'Children of Six Cultures'. It showed how different cultures view the growth and development of children and meet their need to be cared for and nurtured. Whiting compared the way children were reared in six different cultures. He found that in the Philippines, for example, the community believes that maturation* of the child is slow and cannot be hurried. The prevailing belief is that children do not have 'sense' until they are about four years old.

The Khalaphur community in India have a similar philosophy, believing that children *require* protection and physical care until they are about seven years old. In contrast, in some agricultural communities in Kenya, children are expected to take on work responsibilities and help to support their family at the age of six or seven.

However, the beliefs and ideas of a society change over time as its economy develops. The opportunities for children to go to school are now far greater in many developing countries and, therefore, the 'age of reason' arrives earlier. You can compare these examples with your own ideas on childhood from the earlier activity.

The English philosopher John Locke (1632–1704) suggested that the mind of a child was a blank slate upon which experience leaves its impression. This influences the child's future social and moral development. A child who is nurtured in the early years will develop a strong and sensitive personality.

Rousseau, a French philosopher of the eighteenth century, had a different view. He suggested that a person's behavioural patterns are biologically* determined at the moment of conception. This means, for example, that an individual's temperament is genetically* determined by the personality characteristics of both parents, in the same way as one can inherit brown eyes or wavy hair: it's all down to nature and the genes! *

These ideas have been debated for many years amongst childcare and child development experts and have become known as the

Theory

'nature or nurture' debate.

This argument proposes two ideas:

- Behaviour and personality characteristics are inherited from your parents – the nature debate.

- Your behaviour and personality is learnt by social experience – the nurture debate.

The idea that childhood experiences stay with us for a long time is related to these ideas, and was further developed by the psychodynamic* theory of Sigmund Freud.

The psychodynamic theorist would argue that:

- Human behaviour is influenced by the interplay of biological and social factors. In other words, it is the effect of the two working together.

- Human beings change over time as a result of the effect of early relationships with important people in our lives, usually our parents and particularly our mother, to whom we were attached.

John Bowlby (1959–1980) suggested that early experiences of relationships with 'significant others' have long-term implications for a child's future social and emotional development – this is an important area and will be explored further later in the book.

You can now begin to understand that early relationships with significant people are very important to a child's future development. In other words, your child's relationship with you may influence how he/she copes with relationships in the future.

Characteristics: learned or inherited?

Think about the characteristics or similarities you share with your family. As you do this, consider why each person is significant to you.

● What are the qualities you most admire in those people?

● How have they influenced you as you grew up?

What thoughts did you have?

Many children grow up in the knowledge that everyone thinks they are just like their mum, dad, brother, etc. Which is all very well if you happen to think that they are the bee's knees, but what happens if there are dubious skeletons in the closet, or you just don't happen to rate great Uncle Harold as an OK person?

Childhood messages such as 'spare the rod and spoil the child', 'children should be seen and not heard' or 'big boys don't cry, nice glrls don't . . .' are messages about who you are and how you behave that ripple through into adulthood. Different cultures* have different messages.

Discuss

1) What stories or sayings influenced you throughout your childhood?

2) How many times in the last month have you heard yourself sound like your parents, relatives, friends or teachers?

    – What were you saying?
    – Has what you were saying really helped you in the past?

3) What advice have you been given that has helped or hindered you?

    – What did you learn from this?
    – How will this inform the advice you give to your children?
    – *Is* advice *ever useful?*

● 'Some people like my advice so much that they frame it upon the wall instead of using it.'
    Gordon R. Dickson

● 'Good advice is something a man gives when he is too old to set a bad example.'
    Francois de La Rochefoucauld

● 'Advice is what we ask for when we already know the answer but wish we didn't.'
    Erica Jong

● 'It is very difficult to live among people you love and hold back from offering them advice.'
    Anne Tyler

● The true secret of giving advice is, after you have honestly given it, to be perfectly indifferent whether it is taken or not, and never persist in tying to set people right.'
    Hannah Whitall Smith

Familiar sayings

Activity

Tick the sayings that are familiar to you from the list below:

❏   You're just spoilt.

❏   You think we're made of money.

❏   You never do anything to help.

❏   What time do you call this?

❏   I'm sick of hearing… 'It's not fair'.

❏   I'm not wasting money on rubbish like that.

❏   You're not going anywhere until you've eaten it.

❏   You had better clean up your room or else.

❏   Wait until your father gets home.

❏   Go to your bedroom.

❏   I'm always cleaning up after you.

❏   I don't know what you do with your pocket money.

❏   Look at me when I'm talking to you.

❏   I don't care if it's boring.

● How many do you remember hearing as a child, and which do you hear yourself saying now?

● How much did these statements, when they were said to you, influence your behaviour?

Think about

The familiar sayings you remember must have been repeated enough to stay in your memory. You have to decide how useful these ongoing messages are in influencing your own children. If they do have a helpful effect then that's OK, but if not, you could decide to replace these phrases, and any others that you use, for something that is more effective.

The problem with phrases that are frequently repeated is that they don't get heard. You may be accused of nagging. When nagging becomes a habit, it becomes like a TV that is always on but never listened to. However, the original sentiment contained in a phrase may well have been internalised*.

- Are you happy with the childhood messages you are creating for your children?

- Which of your own childhood messages would you want to rewrite?

- And which would you keep?

You have begun to think about your own experiences of being parented as a child. This could be where you learnt how to be, or not to be, a parent yourself. If you did not have a happy childhood then you probably already know what would have helped to make it better. As a child you had very little power to do anything about it. As an adult you can make it different for your children and in so doing, for yourself.

Remembering your childhood

Take some time to complete the following scales and use the ratings to help you think about being a child.

How would you rate your own experiences of:

Being hugged

never										always
0	1	2	3	4	5	6	7	8	9	10

Being praised

never										always
0	1	2	3	4	5	6	7	8	9	10

Being talked with

never										always
0	1	2	3	4	5	6	7	8	9	10

Being listened to

never										always
0	1	2	3	4	5	6	7	8	9	10

Being loved

never										always
0	1	2	3	4	5	6	7	8	9	10

Being valued

never										always
0	1	2	3	4	5	6	7	8	9	10

Looking at your ratings, what do you learn from them that will be useful in bringing up your own children?

Theory

Making memories

Memory is an important part of daily life, influencing every aspect of it. Memory works in a variety of ways, and therefore theorists find it extremely difficult to construct* a single theory to explain all the different aspects of how it works.

'Memories help to . . . place . . . current difficulties in the context of . . . life history. This is important in developing an understanding of how and why [a] person responds and reacts to situations the way they do . . . Memory the psychological research would suggest does not just act as a 'storehouse' of information, but as an active information processing system that as well as storing information, also receives it, stores it and organizes it, alters and recovers it.'

(Wilkinson and Campbell, 1997, page 61)

Some people can remember thousands of things, have an enormous general knowledge, and a wealth of seemingly insignificant trivia stored in their memory. This is selected from their own experiences and is not accessible to others. Though they are able to perform complex and skilled tasks, they find it impossible to remember people's names or birthdays.

The point is that we each store in our memory that which is significant to our lifestyle, or that which is learned because it is repeated often.

Human beings can recall past events in varying degrees of detail, and with a passionate belief in the truth and accuracy of the story. It is possible to believe that a memory is accurate, when in fact it is a distorted version of what happened.

You may have already experienced this when, for example, your child tells you a story about something they remember from their early childhood. This is the "When I was little . . ." story that you recognise – but only in part. It has been stored and organised in your child's memory in a way that is meaningful and significant to them. This is not lying. We all do it. It is how family stories are made, and created, and passed down through generations to become an important part of who we are and what we believe in.

There are many theories of memory. For the purposes of this book we will discuss three of these – 'schema' theory, the 'multi-store' model and the 'working memory'.

Schema theory

Schema theory suggests that what you remember is influenced by what you already know or have experienced. New information is most efficiently remembered when it is hung onto an existing memory or schema*. The knowledge you already have in your memory is organised into schemas or images of what you know.

To illustrate this, consider a child seeing a dog for the first time. He will register a set of information in the brain that identifies that image as a dog. This is a schema, or set of knowledge, about dogs – four legs, tail, fur, whiskers, loud bark.

New information about different 'dogs' will then be managed within this schema, so that over time the child learns that both a Great Dane and a Yorkshire terrier are 'dogs'.

The multi-store model

This model was developed by Atkinson and Shiffrin (1968–1971). The best way to understand this model is to study the following diagram:

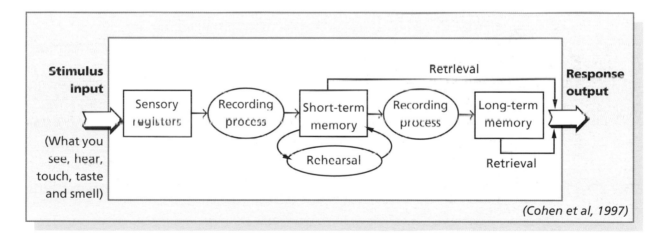

(Cohen et al, 1997)

Try following the diagram using an example – like this:

1. You see something in the environment, like a dog, that is registered by the brain as an asset of shapes and colours. People store their experiences in a number of ways, not only in words but also through pictures and sound. These are known as modalities and are discussed on page 21.

2. The sensory registers – which are a bit like cash registers if you like – record the information (sights, sounds, etc.) and send them to the . . .

Theory

3. . . . short-term memory where they can be recalled when a similar pattern or stimulus is seen or heard (rehearsal) until the information is learned . . .

4. . . . and stored in the long-term memory.

However, short-term memory is much more complicated than the multi-store model! Baddeley and Hitch (1974–1976) suggested that the "working memory is a quick stop-off for information as it journeys towards the long-term memory," and its job is to prepare experiences for storage as long-term memory.

Working memory

The working memory is like an inner voice helping you to prepare experiences that you see and hear, and store them in your long-term memory ready for use. The working memory helps you to store memories or ideas that you have rehearsed in your thoughts, or talked to yourself about – you could be doing this now if you are reading aloud to yourself. You may have heard your child talking her/himself through an activity as s/he attempts to master the skills associated with it, either in learning or play.

So, memories are made and stored through what we see, hear and experience in daily life.

If the learning experience is associated with something impactful*, such as a hurtful, frightening or particularly happy experience, then the memory will be anchored in that stimulus* and can be evoked by the experience at any time. You may not even associate the two things together. So, if a dog bites you, you may become afraid of all things associated with dogs but not necessarily remember being bitten.

Modalities

A person's experience of the world is gathered through different modalities*.

Experiences are stored in our brain as memories. The system is a highly developed onc and we can store memories in different *modalities,* i.e. in different forms.

Let's go back to the example about the dog. The child may see a dog (visual), at the same time hear the name dog (aural*), be encouraged to say the name (oral*) and experience the smell of dog (olfactory*). The child now has a schema of the idea of dog, which has been informed by more than one *modality.* So if the child hears a dog bark but doesn't see it, s/he will know that this is a dog with four legs, tail, fur, whiskers and a loud bark.

Think about

Think of your favourite perfume, music, food, walk, cuddly toy, or item of clothing.

As you think of each of these the smell, look, feel, taste and image come into your mind. The strength of each sensation varies from person to person. So for you a smell may be particularly evocative, e.g. fresh bread; for another person it may be a particular taste or a piece of music.

With memories come associations. These may or may not be pleasant, and can influence your beliefs, actions and attitudes in a way that is not always obvious, and can seem to be quite irrational at times.

If you experienced trauma in your childhood, some experiences trigger memories that can be frightening and unpleasant, even as an adult. This is because they touch the 'child' part of us. Such memories can have a profound effect on relationships, and people can benefit from sensitive counselling to deal with them.

If this is part of your experience then you will be well aware of how important it is to deal with such trauma, and help your children lay down good memories for the future.

Memories can be laid down in a variety of ways, through:

● intense, impactful experiences,

● stories,

● repeated activities, or

● ongoing, shared activity.

As you move through this book, you will explore other ways of helping your children create their future memory bank.

Discuss

- Are people, places, or events most impactful for you?

- What is your earliest childhood memory? Draw a visual impression of it in the box.

- Are you aware of any sounds that are part of your memory? Or smells? Or the feel of something against your skin?

- Is this a good memory?

- Is this a bad memory?

- What is the single most important memory you want your children to have of you when they are grown up?

Psychologists have suggested that children are influenced by the behaviour of others, particularly those who are most important to them (Bandura, 1977). You will be increasingly aware of the importance of sustaining your relationship with your children, even during challenging times. Later you will be considering the effects of bonding and attachment* in families, and it will become apparent how much you do influence your children.

Review

A lot of information has been covered so far. Now is the time to review, and make sense of, the new information you have been considering.

- You unpacked the various images of children and how different cultures maintain different ideas about childhood and children. This helped you to think about your own childhood and your views about your children.

- You considered some theories about how children learn, and were introduced to the idea of socialization.

- We introduced two different views from two philosophers. The first was John Locke who suggested that the child was a blank slate upon which experience leaves its impression. The second was Rousseau who suggested that a person's behavioural patterns are biologically determined at the time of conception.

- You have considered the nature/nurture debate, and formed your own views on how far we inherit or learn various characteristics or behaviours.

- You tried some activities to help you highlight the characteristics, personality, temperament and physiological features within your family.

- You completed an activity enabling you to consider your personal characteristics and how these relate and attach you to your family. With those attachments come histories and belief systems. We will look at this in more detail later.

- You considered some theories about memory and the important role it has to play because it can influence your behaviour and beliefs when associated with early life experiences.

- You have considered how you access the world through your senses (the modalities), and that some smells, tastes, sounds, etc. are particularly evocative. They are even more evocative if the sight, sound or smell is identified or linked with an impactful event.

- Finally we asked you to consider a very important question: what do you want your child to remember about you when they grow up?

Part two

Being a parent

Being a parent

By now you will be aware of some of the reasons why you behave as a parent in the way that you do. This section will explore other influences on your behaviour and moods. You will also reflect on how those early messages percolate through to your relationships in the present. Patterns learnt in childhood can ripple through into your adult responses without you being aware that this has occurred.

So far we have concentrated on life experiences which helped to shape your actions and attitudes. In turn these may have influenced your choices as parents in your management of and hopes for your children.

However, the way that you react in certain situations may also be influenced by external factors – those things over which you have no control. If your response to a situation is reinforced, or noticed and given attention, then it may be repeated again and again. Thus, the behaviour is *learnt*. You can store a learnt pattern in your memory and reproduce it in similar situations which 'stir' those memories or experiences.

If a behaviour or action is repeated over and over, it is said to be *habituated*. It is a *learnt habit*, because it can continue to recur long after the original stimulus or situation has gone. For example, a person may start to bite their nails as a response to a stressful situation, tiredness or boredom. This in turn gives comfort, so the nailbiting is repeated. A habit can develop which may continue long after the original stress or tiredness is gone.

Compare this with your angry reaction to your child's unwanted behaviour. Your child's behaviour may stop as a result, so you try using anger again as a means of controlling his/her behaviour – it stops. This is an interactional pattern that was initially determined by your 'mood'. *This can then be difficult to change, and your child may learn from you that anger is a strategy for coping with frustration.*

Everyone has moods. Some people more than others, depending on personality.

Some people tend to have more happy or 'up' moods; others have more sad or 'down' moods. Moods can reflect the variety of human emotions. They are the outward sign of inward feeling, and an expression of your life experience.

Moods

- Do you have experience of living with someone who is said to be moody?

- How does this affect you and those around you, for example your children?

Their own moods, or those of other people – particularly their parents, can affect children. They can be on a 'high' or a 'low', bad tempered, relaxed or happy.

You know that your child's mood on a particular day will affect his/her performance in school as well as relationships with brothers, sisters and friends.

Children can wake up in a good or bad mood for no apparent reason, but then so can you! Ask your children what makes a good or a bad day.

Think about

What affects your mood and behaviour?

You may have thought of:

- the weather,
- tobacco,
- alcohol,
- money worries,
- relationships,
- environmental factors (noise, smoke, pollen),
- your health,
- conditions at work,
- lack of sleep,
- illness, or
- appearance.

Coping
The interaction* of mood and experience which creates a particular type of behaviour can be called 'coping'.

Everyone experiences some days when they cope better or worse than others. If there are more days when you do not cope well, it's probably time to stop and consider the reasons why this is. What makes a 'coping' day?

Rating scale: coping
How well are you coping?

not well at all									very well indeed	
0	1	2	3	4	5	6	7	8	9	10

Circle on the rating scale how you think you are coping at the moment, and then consider the following questions.

- Are you happy to be at this point on the scale?
- Is this the best/worst you have ever coped?
- How was your life different when you were coping better?
- What is the single change, however small, that would make a difference for the better?
- Where is good *enough* for you, for those around you, for your children?
- What have you learnt about yourself so far to help you cope better?
- Are you moving towards 10, or towards 0?
- Are you content to be at this point?

Your conclusions

So far you have discussed and reflected, considered new ideas and learnt new theory. You have thought carefully and related the theory you have learnt to your own life experience and your observations of others.

You have related your thinking to your own children's experiences. You may already be considering your childhood messages and how they relate to your beliefs about parenting and child development.

You have also had a good hard look at how you are coping on a day-to-day basis. This is not an easy thing to do. Now ask yourself:

● What conclusions have you come to?

● Do you think it is possible for people to change?

● Do you think that it is possible to encourage different behaviour by changing the physical and emotional environment around an individual?

If you think the answer to either of the last two questions is 'no', then you can revisit the previous sections of this book.

Review

Change is possible – it can get better

Do you think people are born with the ability to be a good parent, or do they learn as they go along?

For the purposes of this book we have made some assumptions, which are:

- Skills are honed and developed with experience.

- You have been a child and a parent so you probably know a great deal about the subject already.

- You are the expert on you and also on your child. We say this because you are with your child during good and difficult times.

- In difficult times it feels as though it is like this all the time.

You may wonder why the emphasis has been on you and not your child. The reason for this is based in another principle. This principle is that adults have to get the situation around a child right, to enable the child to function at his/her optimum. Providing the best environment or a 'facilitating environment' (Winnicott, 1990) is important right from birth. Winnicott highlighted the importance of attachment between a child and its carer and referred to the 'environment' as the interdependent relationship between a child and its carer. This is regarded as very important to the future wellbeing of the child and will therefore be explored in more depth later.

In other words, it is your responsibility to organise the circumstances around your child so that he or she can show you his/her best.

Therefore, there are three bases to work from:

- Change is possible.

- To get the best from a child you have to change the situation around him/her.

- The people who know what and how to change a situation are those who are involved.

Review

This book does not aim to diagnose, explain, teach, or prescribe an answer to the challenges you are facing. The examples and ideas used are those that other caring parents have found useful. Our aim is to assist you in actively resolving the problems that you are experiencing in your relationship with your child, or to assist you in deciding to seek further help. Whichever you choose to do, you are in control of the process.

Rating scale: what sort of parent are you?

	not at all					very
Autocratic (bossy)	0	1	2	3	4	5
Laid back	0	1	2	3	4	5
Firm and fair	0	1	2	3	4	5
Even handed	0	1	2	3	4	5
Open to negotiation	0	1	2	3	4	5
'No means no'	0	1	2	3	4	5
Flexible	0	1	2	3	4	5
Consistent	0	1	2	3	4	5
Shout a lot	0	1	2	3	4	5
Always give in	0	1	2	3	4	5
A worrier	0	1	2	3	4	5
An absent parent	0	1	2	3	4	5
A nagging parent	0	1	2	3	4	5
A forgiving parent	0	1	2	3	4	5
A disciplinarian	0	1	2	3	4	5
A friend	0	1	2	3	4	5

Review

- What do you know about yourself that tells you that you are, or can be, a good parent?

- What parts of your parenting style do you want to change?

- What parts of your parenting style, either shown on the rating or other parts that you can think of, are you most happy with?

- If you asked your partner, neighbour or mother what impressed them about you as a parent, what would they say?

- Which rating are you most pleased about?

- Which styles do you wish to use more in your future efforts as a parent?

- What do you most want your children to remember when they are parents?

- Do you think that the style of parenting you experienced as a child was similar to your current style?

- Are there any styles of parenting missing from the list above?

Thank you for completing this rating. If it has been a useful exercise you may want to refer to it again. Why not get a copy and complete it with a partner or friend, or perhaps your children? The feedback you get may be interesting and help you to resolve your concerns. Sometimes other people can see what you can't; their opinions can act like a mirror and enable you to see yourself the way others see you.

Part three

Bonding and attachment

Bonding and attachment

In every culture, importance is given to the relationship between a child and his/her parent/carer.

You may remember that 'bonding' was discussed when you were waiting for your child(ren) to arrive, or shortly after the birth. The notion of bonding* is usually associated with mother and baby, and it is known to occur in the human and animal kingdoms.

Bonding is described as the rush of feeling that comes when you see your child, perhaps for the first time. Do you remember it? You may also remember the way that your baby gazed at you for long periods of time when you were feeding him/her – in some parts of the country this is known as 'looking babies'. There are many activities that enable bonding to occur when your baby is very young because (s)he is so dependent on you, and you are constantly engaged in close physical contact.

Attachment occurs in three distinct phases and these are:

1) the initial trust a child develops in his/her parent – the bond is evident in the first six months. If separation occurs after this, the child has to transfer the attachment to another carer. The child may not trust that his needs will be met consistently.

2) the communication between the child and his/her parent/carer which illustrates that the child is a special person. This occurs in play and when caring for a child's physical needs. Feeding, talking, cuddling, reading, singing or laughing with a child and the efforts to soothe or comfort a frustrated or ill child will develop this bond.

3) recognition of the child's individual place in its family or community. This event is often ritualised into a formal ceremony, which is different in every culture. You may be familiar with the Sikh naming ceremony when the child's name is made public in the Gurdwara, or the Christian baptismal ceremony when the child is blessed with holy water.

Children and carers

The importance of the relationship between a child and its mother (or primary carer) has long been understood. Donald Winnicott, a paediatrician and psychoanalyst, described the need of the child to experience total dependence on its carer until such time as the child resists them to emerge as a separate and psychologically complete being. He observed that there is no such thing as a baby, only 'a baby and someone' (cited in McMahon, page 3). Children who have experienced a 'good enough' early environment (i.e. adequate nurturing and experience of independence) will develop to become children and adults who cope and manage more effectively. (Winnicott, 1963).

Activity

Closeness

- Can you recall some of the times when you felt closest to your child?

- Ask your partner when s/he has felt close to your child.

- Talk to your child about when they felt close to you.

This activity will be very easy for some parents. They can look back on the early days of their parenting with real fondness and pleasure. They easily recall activities with their children, such as painting, running in the garden, cuddling or rough and tumble together.

Some parents find it very easy to recall their baby's first tooth, steps, solid food, haircut and a myriad of events that can leave other parents bemused, and perhaps feeling a bit inadequate.

However, it is important to understand that parenthood is not the same for everyone. Not everyone feels terribly intense about his or her children from day one.

Many factors can interfere with this process, and they affect a surprising number of people. Such factors can be:

- an unplanned pregnancy,
- a bad pregnancy when you were continually ill,
- a traumatic or early birth,
- postnatal depression,
- relationship difficulties,
- social difficulties, e.g. poor housing,
- financial problems,
- a challenging baby, e.g. a baby who doesn't feed, has colic or doesn't sleep.

Any number of factors can interfere with a developing relationship between children and parents. As long ago as 1967, in a research study of patients' records linking stressful life events and illness, Holmes and Rahe identified 43 stressful life events including some of those mentioned above.

Activity

Rating Scale: bonding
1) How well did you bond with your baby?

| not very well | | | | | | | | | | | | | | | | | | | very well |

1 2 3 4 5 6 7 8 9 10 11 12 13 14 15 16 17 18 19 20

You may want to take a few minutes to think about this and discuss your conclusions with a partner or friend.

- Ask them if they agree with your rating.
- Do they rate you higher or lower?
- What did they see you do that made them decide to give you this rating?
- Are you surprised?

Take some time to think about your rating.

- How did you come to this decision?
- Is your rating high or low?
- Are you happy with your rating, and how you bonded with your baby?
- What did you think about when you gave yourself this rating? Why did you not give yourself a lower rating?
- What specific experiences resulted in the attachment that you now have with your child?

2) How well have you bonded with your child now?

| not very well | | | | | | | | | | | | | | | | | | | very well |

1 2 3 4 5 6 7 8 9 10 11 12 13 14 15 16 17 18 19 20

Now ask yourself the same questions as before. Share your conclusions with your partner or a friend.

Thinking of these things can be a difficult and even emotional experience. You could begin to blame others or yourself, when it may be that circumstances have been against you.

However, the bonding that occurred early in your relationship with your child is not *fixed*. Attachments can change. You can feel closer to, or further away from, your children at different points in time. Remember, change is possible.

Think about

Loving and liking

Some people say that it is possible to love your child but not like them very much. Do you think this is true?

These are not unusual feelings. It is likely that you experience them in other relationships you have, but that you, like most people, learn to 'manage' them. Remember, you have already learnt that the way you manage relationships as adults is influenced by your own early life experiences.

Having thought carefully about the influences in your own early life, you can begin to rethink your hopes for your children, and become aware of just how much influence you have on them.

Many parents and carers tell us that their relationship with their child has changed over time. Early, very close bonding that does not develop to meet adults' and child's needs will be suffocating and restrictive. Alternatively, a once close bond can be stressed when a child seeks increasing independence or autonomy, or challenges the bonds with confusing behaviour.

Ironically, if you asked your child how close they felt to you they would probably give a much higher rating than you, even when things are bad. Yet at times it feels absolutely the opposite – it may even feel as if your child is punishing you. If you have teenagers, you may sometimes feel as if you have lost all communication with them.

Remember that your child is 'programmed' to have an attachment to a main carer. Their experience of being attached is different to yours because it is based on their dependence on you.

If you feel that your bond with your child is not as close as you would like, it is probably time to do something about it.

Remember, you are the adult. You have more control and power over the situation, and more wisdom. It is your responsibility to manage the situation. Usually it is unhelpful to start by demanding that the child changes first. Yet people often do.

1 The notion of *responsibility* is one of the principles of this book. According to British law, parental responsibility means all the rights, duties, powers, responsibilities, and authority, which by law the parent of a child has in relation to the child and his property. (Nick Allen, 1993).

However, we are not only talking about legal responsibility here[1]. We are referring to the responsibility of love and commitment that parents make to their children, and their responsibility to ensure that their children grow up to be emotionally healthy and resilient. You have already acknowledged your responsibility by beginning to do something about your concerns.

Play and communication – emotional glue

If there are relationship issues between you and your child, or if your attachment is not as close as you would wish, then shared activities which give mutual enjoyment can provide emotional glue*.

"Human emotions are interactive in that our emotion when perceived by another can change that person's feelings and motives. Emotions of pleasure and excitement provide the vital emotional 'glue' to maintain interaction."

(Trevarthen, 1992)

Consider for a moment what this statement means to you.

- Can you identify the emotional glue in your own life? Discuss this in your group, or with your partner or mentor.

- If you agree with this statement, what actions can you take to develop 'emotional glue' in your own family?

- What will you do to continue to provide emotional glue?

Sustaining relationships

When you are challenged by your children's behaviour, playing with them can become a chore. Providing activities to share pleasure and excitement can feel like a waste of time if they end in tears.

"Will you play with me . . ." can evoke a groan from frustrated and tired parents. Alternatively, if you offer to play with your child and they reply "no thanks", this can feel like a rejection. If you do feel rejected in this situation, it may be due to an earlier life experience, or as a result of a long-term memory that has been stimulated (as discussed in part 1). However, your child's response could be attributed to their mood or previous unsatisfying experiences. They may even feel that it is just as inconvenient to them as it was to you the last time they asked you to play.

Learning to play with children is a skill involving communication, creativity, learning and teaching, having fun, and, most of all, creating and cementing a special relationship.

Activity

Remembering playing

1) Think about your early childhood and how you played with other children, teachers, parents and significant adults in your life.

- You may have been left to play alone. How did that feel?

- It may be that you were deprived of quality time to play. How do you feel about that now?

- Will these memories help you to do things with your own children that you never did as a child?

2) Think about a play memory you have from childhood.

- What made this particular experience a good or bad one?

- Did this experience build upon your attachment to the person you were playing with?

- If it was a good experience, identify the 'emotional glue' that was created.

- How will you use what you now know with your own children?

Play and co-operation

Research has indicated that children whose parents encouraged them to play with other children, and provided games involving co-operation, tended to become popular with others (Harper, L. and Huie, K., 1985). Later research showed that children working co-operatively, for example on computers, made significantly more progress than children working alone (Me Varech, Z.,1991).

Ask your child's teacher what their experience of children working in groups is, and if they agree with the findings of Me Varech.

Through play and friendships children learn about themselves, other people, how the social world operates, and about status and fairness in relationships. But, there are other important effects of play and communication. The work of Russian psychologist Vygotsky (1933) and social psychologist George Herbert Mead (1934) indicated that play offers children the chance to manipulate and test out rules for social interaction. Concepts, language, attention and memory skills are all developed through play between a child and another person. However, play stimulates learning and reinforces relationships.

It is obvious that play is important as it enables children to experience the world, develop social skills, language skills and vocabulary, and learn to understand other people. Therefore, the more play opportunities you have with your children, the more influence you have as you encourage them to develop in a way that you consider to be appropriate.

The activities you share with older children and teenagers may be different, but the purpose is the same – to stimulate your child's learning, increase shared experiences and, subsequently, your understanding of each other. As older children increasingly seek the company of their peers, maintaining communication through shared activities is an invaluable way of sustaining your relationship. Some ideas for play and shared activities can be found on page 46.

Remember:

- that if you 'bank-up' enough shared times with your children, they are more likely to accept those times when you cannot, or do not, feel like playing with them.

- the theme of this book – you know what it is like to be a child. You have been there and done it. So, when you do this exercise it is helpful to think about when you were younger.

Activity

A questionnaire

Complete this by yourself or with others. When you have finished you may wish to discuss some of the alternatives given and add some of your own.

1) You have just come in from work. You are tired, have had a lousy day, and got stuck in traffic on the way home. Your teenager wants to play a game on the computer with you. What do you do?
   - Groan and comply.
   - Tell them to make a coffee whilst you get changed and then you will have ten minutes.
   - Ignore him and start making the tea.
   - Ignore him and read the paper.

2) You are visiting a friend with your children. Your children are being incredibly noisy and are interrupting your conversation. You know it is because they are bored. What do you do?
   - Apologise to your friend and say how embarrassed you are by your children.
   - Tear a strip off them and threaten them with early bed.
   - Join in the play for a time, and put in some controls.
   - Give up the visit and come back when they are at school.

3) It's your daughter's birthday and you have planned a party for 10 children in the garden. It pours with rain. What do you do?
   - Cancel the party.
   - Adjourn to the burger bar with money you had saved from the family allowance, just in case.
   - Play outside anyway.
   - Enlist the help of their mums and dads and have a disco in the house.

4) You have planned a trip to the park. When you are ready to leave, your children's friends turn up. They don't want to go to the park because "it's boring". What do you do?
   - Go anyway and take their friends.
   - Have a picnic at home instead.
   - Send their friends home and go to the park.
   - Feel very annoyed; give your children a long lecture on how they complain you never do anything with them, and when you do look what happens.

5) Your son's friend always has sleepovers with videos and expensive treats for 4 or 5 children. You can't do that because you haven't got the room and you can't afford it. What do you do?
   - Ban your son from ever attending anyone's sleepover.
   - Do it once in a while, when you can afford it.
   - Ask you son's friend's parents not to invite him any more.

- Think up an alternative activity involving fewer bought treats.

6) You are planning your holiday. Do you:
- Look for somewhere with a Kids Club running activities 12 hours a day – after all this is your annual holiday.
- Look for somewhere with activities for all ages that can be shared.
- Take grandma.
- Take a friend for each child.

7) It's Christmas. Do you:
- Watch your children open all their presents, and then leave them to get on with it.
- Watch them open all their presents, and sleep all afternoon.
- Set some time aside to play with the new toys.
- Leave Uncle to play with your children and their new toys while you stuff the turkey.

8) You are on a day out as a family. Which is your most demanding activity:
- Doling out food.
- Doling out money.
- Waiting whilst your children are on the rides.
- Making sure you have a go on everything.

These are some of the situations that can be so difficult to manage. They can lead to real rows between you and your children, and the use of that well-worn phrase, "It's not fair!" Repeating these conflicting experiences will affect the relationship between you and your children and other relationships within your family – particularly if adults quarrel about how a situation should be managed. This can be the beginning of a loop of conflict within your family, which alters the relationships within it and causes emotional distress. There is more information about this in part 5.

Now review your answers. There are no right or wrong ones, but considering the alternatives offered will help you choose the most effective response for you.

What do your responses suggest to you? How else could you deal with these situations?

What would you have liked your mum, dad, aunt, grandma, or whoever cared for you to do in these situations?

Work through the questions with a friend or partner and discuss what you would do in each situation. Based on what you know already, which choices would you not make?

Think about

Shared activities

Think about times when you have shared activities with your child.

- What did you both enjoy, or dislike, about the activity?
- What difference did it make to your relationship, i.e. did it make you feel closer to your child?
- Which shared activities – enjoyed by both yourself and your child(ren) – could you usefully repeat to increase your family's emotional glue?
- Ask your child which activities they like best, and which could become favourites.
- Which activities have been most rewarding
    - for you?
    - for your children?
    - for your partner?
    - for your family?

You could rate your activities on a scale of 0–5 like this:

0	1	2	3	4	5

liked least *liked most*

Try this rating scale with younger children:

liked least *liked most*

As an expert open to continued learning, you are exploring ways in which you, your child and your family benefit socially, emotionally and educationally from shared activities.

Shared activities can provide a range of benefits for you and your children: bringing you closer as a family, improving communication and relationships. However, sharing activities can be stressful when there are competing demands, for example on a family holiday. This is when all your negotiation, diplomacy, and conflict resolution skills come to the fore!

However, if your time is given grudgingly then activities become a chore. Similarly, if the activity is boring or unsuitable to your child then the benefits will be lost. It is a good idea to divide activities with a partner so that each parent/carer has special time with the children.

Organising activities when families are separated takes sophisticated planning! If children do not live with a parent, then special time for activities both outside and inside the home are important. As is time for:

- exchange of news,
- giving and receiving of praise,
- relaxing time,
- bonding time,
- teaching time,
- learning time, and
- fun time.

If these activities are given due priority, then difficult times may not seem so bad.

Adults very often use activities as a reward for good behaviour. If your child is challenging it can be tempting to make your time conditional* on good behaviour. Psychologists call the rewarding or punishing of behaviour 'behaviour modification'*.

There are pros and cons to rewarding children with attention and withdrawing it as a punishment. On balance it is likely that most activities earned by 'being good' lose their appeal. So, the subsequent strengthening of the parent-child relationship does not occur in the same way it does if your time is given freely and unconditionally because you want to be with your children. The rewards are there for you too.

As you begin to use the knowledge you have about being a child, the more rewarding it becomes to have time with your child(ren). You begin to enjoy the opportunity to observe your child(ren) grow, developing physically and in their skills and attitudes. The more time you can offer to your child the more you deposit in your 'influence bank' to be drawn on now or later.

"We can appreciate moments of connecting with a child. We can enter a child's world. Sitting down on the floor to play a game of jacks with a five-year old. Sharing the delight of a three-year old who has just discovered how to smell a flower. Building a palace of wooden blocks — enjoy the crash as they tumble to the ground. Joining the thrill of a six-year old who has just learnt how to ride a bicycle. It's never too late to have fun with kids and extend your own childhood, happily."

(Furman, page 58)

After all, it won't be long before your children's memories of what they did with you are stories to pass on to their children.

Activity

Ideas for shared activities

Activity	Age	Benefits
Swimming	Any age from a few months	Physical exercise, fun, develops motor skills, relaxing, burns off energy, opportunity for physical contact.
Ball games	Any age when mobile	Develops co-ordination, gross motor skills, teamwork, competitiveness.
Dressing-up, pretend play	Any age when mobile	Imagination, role-play, empathy.
Cooking, crafts, water play	Any age when mobile	Fine and gross motor skills, language.
Reading, art, computers	4 years onwards	Develops fine motor skills, imagination, concentration, vocabulary, discussion.
Fishing, model making, collecting	7 years onwards	Concentration, patience, general knowledge.
Scrabble, jigsaws, board games	7 years onwards	Turn-taking, patience, reasoning.
Bowling, snooker	Teens	Relaxing, meeting with like-minded others, turn-taking, conversation, self-esteem through approval and achievement.

This list is not exhaustive: think of your own ideas to add to it.

A metaphor* – highs and lows

Life in families has its ups and downs. When in a 'down' it can be difficult to see the 'up' or to tell yourself this is a phase that will pass. The reading and thinking you have undertaken up to this point may leave you hopeful or cynical, but we are not aiming to give an impression that this is all easy or enormously difficult. It might be helpful to take a break here and think about your current situation within a larger view of what is happening and has happened in your life. We are including an analogy at this point which might help you to do this.

Think of a grandfather or pendulum clock. The pendulum swings to and fro powering the hands of the clock to mark the passing of time.

The rise and fall of the pendulum can be likened to the ups and downs of life. Regardless of whether life is in a up or a down, time rolls on. In other words this time will pass . . . unless you stop trying.

Everyone experiences highs and lows, and sometimes it can feel as if you are stuck. However, as with the pendulum, a little nudge in the right direction can start the movement again and prompt change.

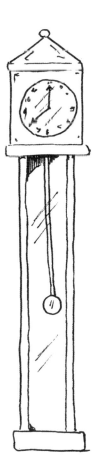

Think about

How might this apply to your own situation?

● What are your highs and lows?
● When are you stuck?
● What do you need to do to give a little nudge?

Think about how this can apply to you, your partner, and your children. In the next section there are some tips about nudging a stuck situation.

Banking time and listening

Finding the right way to 'give a little nudge' to a stuck situation can be easier said than done.

If you bank up enough shared times then the times you cannot, or do not feel like playing or spending 'quality time' are more likely to be accepted by your children.

Time with children does not have to be playing time. It is equally important to have talking and listening time together. You will have heard a variety of adults attempt to sort out a difficulty by 'talking to' the child. As a first resort, children are very often given a 'talking to'. You may have already tried this, and must decide for yourself how successful it was.

You must not forget the effect of listening to your children.

This sounds easy but is difficult to do without real awareness and effort on your part. Many adults have to consciously remember to ask how their child's day has been and to follow-up with a focused question if a long and elaborate story has been shared in the middle of a favourite soap, conversation with a neighbour or when out shopping. You will recall from part one that new experiences are hung on a framework created by old ones and woven together to create a meaningful story.

Perhaps now is a good time to make a resolution to listen to your children at least once every day, and tell them that you have really tried to understand the importance of what they are telling you. On the next page we have included a sheet to record those things that you are proud of doing. It is likely to be those things that provide the 'nudge' mentioned earlier. You can use this sheet in a way that is most helpful to you. For example, you could decide to record those things you notice your child doing that make you feel proud – particularly if these are things that your child has learned or absorbed from you. Children are influenced by those who care for them and share their experiences.

I am proud because I . . .

Monday
_____
_____
_____

Tuesday
_____
_____
_____

Wednesday
_____
_____
_____

Thursday
_____
_____
_____

Friday
_____
_____
_____

Saturday
_____
_____
_____

Sunday
_____
_____
_____

This week I noticed I can
_____
_____
_____
_____

Talking with children

Talking with children rather than to them is a skilful activity. Many people say they will have a *talk to* a child about an issue, but having the time and patience to untangle a complex story and *talk about* it, is a different skill.

You may have noticed some or all of the following when chatting with your children:

- They may not communicate in full sentences, or with the logical sequence of a story using a beginning, middle and an end.

- They leave bits in and take bits out – they are selective in what they tell and find interesting.

- They remind you about things they told you last week, yet you have no recollection of the conversation.

- They do not voluntarily tell you the things you really want to know, for example if they got 7 out of 10 for spelling, what did their friend get?

- You sometimes feel that they are not telling you the truth because what they are saying doesn't make sense to you.

This happens because children acquire language, and the ability to use it effectively, at different ages and stages. The stage that most people recognise is the teenager, who seems to lose the power of language for a time and communicate only in grunts, groans and body language!

Nevertheless, don't give up!

You must encourage children to tell you the least important parts of their day, so that they feel confident enough to tell you about their most important parts.

Good communication with your children does not only happen through verbal language. You can communicate your attachment, approval, affection and aspirations in many different ways through the day-to-day tasks you undertake for them.

Nurturing

- How willingly do you undertake the daily chores associated with the care of your children?

0	1	2	3	4	5	6	7	8	9	10

unwillingly   *very willingly*

You probably enjoy some of these daily chores but not others. Talk about which chores you enjoy, and how you can make those you dislike more enjoyable.

Do you share your daily chores with anyone? Is there anyone who can help you with the chores that you don't like? Even occasional help can give you a break and may help you to enjoy your other tasks more.

Caring for someone with real commitment enables that person to feel nurtured and important, and enhance his or her self-esteem. It is a very important bonding experience for children. This applies whether the carer is male or female.

Review

What you know now and what others have written

This section has focused on you and what you know. You may be encouraged to find ways of managing your relationship with your child that stem from your own experience of being a child. At the beginning of the chapter you made a decision that change was possible, and you were prepared to consider what differences you might make in your relationship with your children.

You also looked at your moods and coping skills, and how you want to extend your existing talents as a parent to develop new skills based on previous experiences.

Having recalled your early experiences and relationships, you have explored theories of bonding and attachment, and how you can strengthen and sustain the attachments between yourself and your child through communication, play and shared activities, banking special time and communication. Even if your own early attachments were broken or weakened, you will understand the importance of strengthening your future bonds with your children.

Shared activities, banking time and listening help to increase attachments. If you have increased the activities you share in your family then congratulations to you. If this is something that you still have to work on then you may choose to revisit the section.

As you increase the quality time you spend with your children, it is important to understand their stages of development and enhance communication through the use of language and play. This is such an important area that we will be giving it further consideration, from a different theoretical perspective, in the next part of this book.

To end this section and draw it to a close you might like to think about these comments from other writers in the field of childcare:

'Our past is a story we can tell ourselves in many different ways. By paying attention to methods that have helped us survive, we can start respecting ourselves and reminiscing about our difficult past with feelings of pride rather than regret.'

(Furman, page 56)

'I don't think it's ever too late to have a happy childhood. I don't think we ever lose our childlike eyes, really. In fact, it's when we deny their curiosity and desire for growth and learning that we become our troubled past. Then we allow it to lead us through troubled lives with excuses of why we can't …Perhaps the key to a more fulfilling life may not be in searching for stress relievers, happiness or peace, but in placing ourselves in the environments that encourage childlike joy.'

(Metcalfe in Furman op cit)

Part four

Communicating with each other

Communicating with each other

In this section we will focus on the importance of effective communication between family members. This includes:

- how people let each other know how they are feeling,
- what they think about shared issues, or
- why they are behaving in certain ways.

We will discuss a model that describes and explains human behaviour from a psychotherapeutic* perspective. This model is called 'transactional analysis'.

The ideas referred to here have been used by psychologists, psychiatrists, psychotherapists and counsellors over many years. We have chosen to include this model because it has helped us find effective ways to help many families. If you decide to seek professional help, the person you see may be influenced by this model.

Transactional analysis

A useful model to help people think about how they communicate with each other is based on the work of Eric Berne (1910–1970) an eminent psychiatrist and psychoanalyst.

His theory maintains that people have within them *ego* states,* or ways of being and feeling, which influence their feelings about relationships, and how relationships can modify their behaviour and interactions. This idea pre-dates Berne and is linked to the nineteenth century work of Freud.

Berne proposed that all people, regardless of age or development, carry within them three *ego states.* At any given moment a person will display one or other of these states when interacting with others. The states are:

Parental ego state
A set of feelings, thoughts and behaviour resembling those of parental figures.

Adult ego state
An adult ego state autonomously and objectively appraises reality and makes judgements. It is recognised by its organisation, adaptability and intelligence.

Child ego state
A child ego state represents feelings, thoughts and actions that are left over from childhood. Berne's theory says that everyone carries a child within them

- Does this make sense to you? Can you identify with the ego states described here?

Activity

Understanding ego states

In each box, give an example of the behaviour or language you think might be typical of each ego state. Compare with your partner, others in your group, or discuss with your mentor.

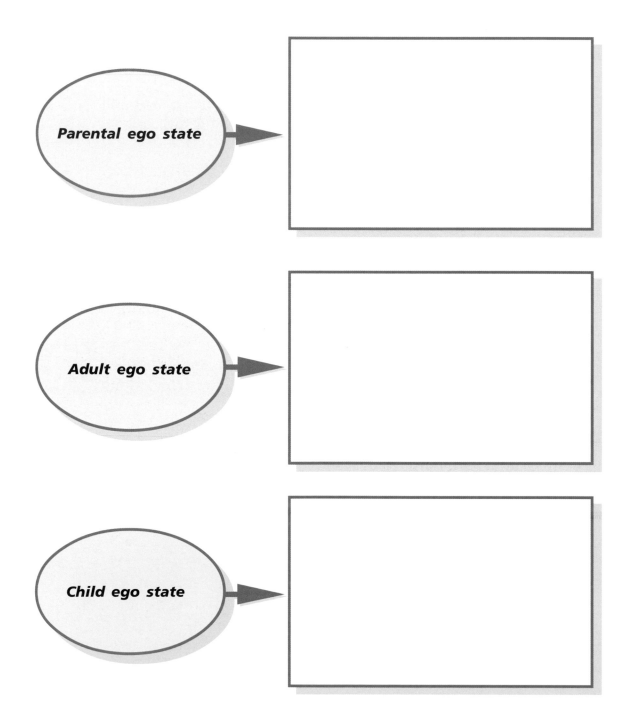

Parental ego state

Adult ego state

Child ego state

Each ego state has within it a range of characteristics which can be positive or negative. Compare the definitions below with what you have just written or discussed.

Critical parent

Can be over controlling and inhibit growth. The controlling parent is inflexible and is recognised by a set of arbitrary and rigid rules.

Nurturing parent

The nurturing parent shows a sympathetic, caring attitude towards another individual. They can be supportive and enhance growth.

Adult ego state

A person in an adult ego state is calm, logical, rational and consistent.

Free child

The free child shows feelings and behaviour that can be influenced by their parent/carer. They can also respond with non-compliance or sulking, although they are usually creative and fun. Another term for the free child is the adapted child.

Rebellious child

The rebellious child displays behaviour such as spontaneous expression, non-compliance, creativity, challenge or rebellion. Another term for the rebellious child is the natural child.

Activity

Identifying ego states

Can you identify the predominant ego states in each example?

Example 1: An accident in the garden

Imagine that you went into the garden, stepped on a rake and hurt yourself. Below are some of the ways you might react. Can you identify the ego state that is predominant in each example?

A) Go inside complaining that some stupid person left the rake out. Although you have told them a million times to put things away, they never learn.

B) Go inside in a rage, and shout at everyone in sight.

C) Go inside and ask who forgot to take the rake in. Explain that it was left outside, and you have hurt yourself on it. Suggest that, for everyone's future safety, it would be better if we were all more careful.

Answers		
A) critical parent	B) rebellious child	C) adult

Example 2: Sibling rivalry

Imagine this scenario in the home.

A) Father: "Jamie, pass the books here please: I don't want anyone to trip on them."

B) Jamie: "In a minute: I'm in a good bit of my game."

C) Father: "Why can you never do as you're told when you're asked? It's always the same. I said, do it now."

D) Jamie: "Why don't you ask her? Little Miss Goody. You never ask her. It's not fair."

E) Father: "Well, if you helped round here once in a while you wouldn't get told all the time. DO IT NOW."

F) Little sister: "I'll do it, daddy."

G) "Aaah! There's a good girl!"

Answers		
A) adult	B) free child	C) critical parent
D) rebellious child	E) critical parent	F) free child
	G) nurturing parent if said by father, but could be an ulterior transaction if said by Jamie (see page 63)	

Example 3: A day out

Imagine that you are driving, in moderately heavy traffic, with your family in the car. You and your partner are discussing the best dates for a holiday, and have just worked them out.

A) Another car overtakes you, without warning and seemingly unnecessarily. You are really angry, make rude gestures and shout out of the window, mouthing at the passing driver.

B) Your partner tells you to calm down: some people are really silly and it's not worth getting upset about.

C) You ask your partner who is driving this car. If they are so sure that they can do better with such idiots on the road, they should try.

D) Your partner responds that s/he will just shut up then, since you know it all.

E) You continue the journey in silence, until your young son asks why you stopped talking about the holiday.

Answers

A) rebellious child
B) nurturing parent
C) rebellious child
D) rebellious child
E) adult

Applying transactional analysis at home

Can you recognise, in yourself or someone else, the different characteristics that Berne is referring too?

● Which is the predominant characteristic that you see in yourself?

● What is the most obvious characteristic you see in:

– your child?

– your partner?

– those around you?

This model is very useful because if you begin to understand and recognise the characteristics of an ego state, it is possible to work out what you need to do to improve your communication with others – you will be aware of the *transactions* between people.

Now try analysing the relationships of a family in one of your favourite soap operas.

The transactional analysis model is very useful in helping you understand what people might be feeling in a conversation or exchange. It is a good idea to 'be curious' about how a person might be feeling during a conversation and this will assist in modifying your own response to get the best outcome from the conversation.

Transactions

Within this theory, a *transaction* is a communication that occurs between people. There are three main types of transactions:

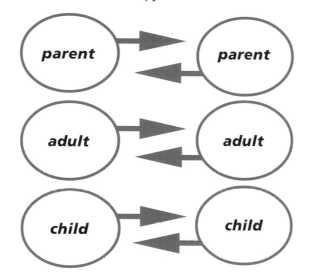

These are 'complementary transactions', where a communication is given and responded to from the same ego state.

So, for example,

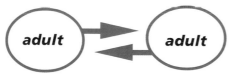

Husband: "Are you cold dear?"
Wife: "No dear, are you?"

1) Is this a nurturing or critical parent ego state?

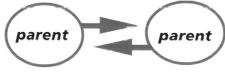

Husband: "It's cold in here."
Wife: "That's because the heating isn't on."

2) What makes this an adult to adult interaction?

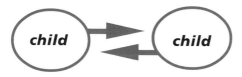

Husband: "I'm freezing in here."
Wife: "So what . . ."

3) There are two ego states displayed here. Can you identify them?

Answers

1) nurturing parent   2) because a logical response is given to a statement
3) husband and wife are both displaying the ego state of a rebellious child

Theory

Crossed transactions

This is where a communication is given from one ego state, but received and responded to in another.

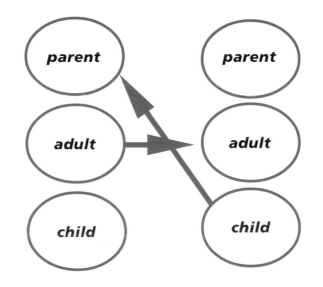

For example,

Husband: "It's cold in here." (adult)
Wife: "Get a cardigan then, dear." (nurturing parent)

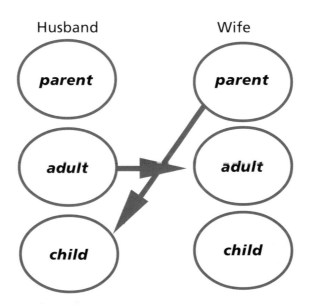

In this example, you will see that the husband is making a factual statement about the temperature of the room, which is cold. If it is a fact, this makes it an adult statement.

The wife responds with words that can be perceived as nurturing, because she is giving advice and offering an endearment.

But . . .

If the tone of voice in which this conversation occurs is harsh, the transaction is *changed* and could become a squabble – child to child, or critical parent to adult. The interaction is altered by the intonation.

Ulterior transactions

An ulterior transaction occurs when a communication is meant one way but is said in another.

A good example of this is the use of sarcasm – "Well *aren't* you a good boy!" Here the words indicate one statement but the tone another.

In diagram form, an ulterior transaction might look like the illustration below.

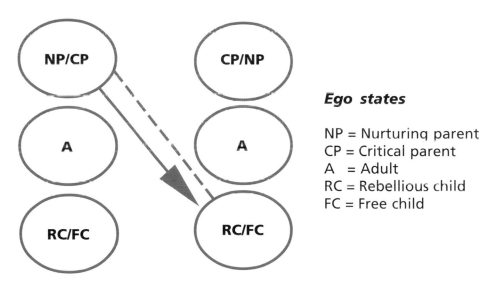

Ego states

NP = Nurturing parent
CP = Critical parent
A = Adult
RC = Rebellious child
FC = Free child

When a crossed or ulterior transaction occurs, communication is broken-off and becomes ineffective.

An ulterior transaction can be damaging, and, when used with your children as a means of controlling them, can lead to major arguments. This is because a young child becomes confused with the messages he has been given, and therefore cannot be sure what he has to do to please you.

An older child or teenager may well respond from an ego state that you did not expect and cannot handle.

Review

When you begin to think about how we communicate daily, you can see how useful this model can be as a way of thinking about how we communicate with our children.

- Some complex ideas about transactional analysis have been explored in this last section.

- Discuss with your partner, friend or mentor what you have learnt from this section.

- If you are interested in reading and developing these ideas further, you will find useful references in the Bibliography at the back of this book.

- Has this chapter helped you to think about communication between people, and how it enables behaviour and relationships to develop, or become stuck?

- When you become aware of how easily people move in and out of ego states, then understanding a conversation becomes a whole new experience. We hope this has helped to move your thinking a step further.

Part five

Families . . . and living in them

Families . . . and living in them

Having considered the significance of verbal and nonverbal communication (e.g. body language) and how this can influence your relationships, it will be useful to consider some theory about families and how they function.

You have already been able to make some changes in your relationship with your child(ren). In this part of this book, you will be able to continue developing skills to enable those changes to grow and become established. The changes will therefore, be sustained, and the attachments established on a stronger basis.

Relationships within your family are central to the wellbeing of your children. You will now explore some theory related to family structures and belief systems.

Families

The middle decades of the last century have imprinted on our minds the idea of a 'nuclear' family that is now more of a stereotype. Families are no longer solely made up of mother, father, two children, home and dog. Families can consist of same sex parents, parents of different ethnic backgrounds with dual heritage children, birth parents or adoptive carers. Families can be transgenerational (i.e. there are more than two generations in the home); there can be no income or multi-incomes. This means that a child may have friends whose families are not like his/her own and so, from an early age, may feel the considerable impact of *difference*.

Family structures change over time, so when we refer to a 'family' it means *your* family. However, there are some definitions that help to define the changing structure of families. Here is one example:

'A family with dependent children is a group in which one or more adults cares for the children and expects to do so until the children are no longer dependent.

The children may or may not be biologically related to the adult or adults. If there are two adults they may be a married couple or cohabiting heterosexual or homosexual couple; they may be foster parents adoptive parents, a step parent and parent, grandparents or other relations. If there is one adult that person may be a biological parent to the children or a foster parent, grandparent or other relative. The children may not live in one family household all of the time, but between one another frequently or occasionally.'

(Batchelor et al., 1994, page 9–10)

Changing family structures are inevitable. They are determined by economic, political and technological advances, all of which have a significant impact on your health and wellbeing, and your relationships. The twentieth century was unique in its speed of change, which, in turn, brought stresses and challenges to individuals.

However, most children will be born into a family unit, which is where s/he will be nurtured for at least the early parts of her/his life.

Relationships bring warmth, consistency and stability to people's lives. By now you will be aware of the most important relationships throughout your own life, and those that are most important to you at the moment.

The most enduring relationships are those between children and parents. It is within the family that children learn to manage emotional climates, in preparation for future life.

Children are often the barometers* of the family's emotional climate. Stresses and tensions in the home, or in adults, can at times show themselves in the behaviour of the children. This can be noticed by those around the child, such as teachers and neighbours, but missed, or seen as 'naughtiness', by parents/carers who are preoccupied with adult relationships.

Most people engaged in childcare need the benefit of a supportive relationship with which to manage life's stresses. A study carried out in South London (Brown and Harris, 1978) found that women who had experienced stressful events and circumstances in their lives were less likely to experience depression if they had a partner to share it with.

This is confirmed by later studies (Miell and Dallas, 1996) who found that: "Close relationships are particularly important for mental health; social support has a buffering effect on stress."

Families: well-oiled machines?

Family therapists, and others who work with families, view the family as a system*. We use the analogy of a machine, made up of a number of interacting parts or cogs. The smooth running of the machine largely depends on each component part fulfilling its role and function. If one cog or part of the system is removed, or malfunctions, then this puts pressure on other parts of the machine or system.

What of those parents who are rearing children alone? People have for some years been aware of the effects of separation and divorce on children and families (De'Ath and Slater, 1992), when the family machine has to reorganize itself around an unsettling event. A family member leaving the home (for whatever reason) can unsettle the family balance, causing roles and relationships to change. Take, for example, a father moving out of the family home, leaving his oldest son in charge. The son may see his role as 'looking after mum', and being 'the man of the house'. This will affect the relationship between the son and his mother, and probably between the son and the other siblings* too.

Similarly, when an older sibling leaves home, a younger sibling achieves a more senior status. Behaviour can change to accommodate this difference.

Another example is if a mother is away from home. She may be working, hospitalised or absent for some other reason. There can be a profound effect on the emotional climate in the household if, for example, a daughter has to take on the role and duties of mum or father and sons are left alone. This means that, as the family is adapting to change, the remaining parent has to accommodate and buffer the alterations in roles and relationships, without the beneficial support of their partner. This may affect the relationship of the adults, and in turn impact on the children.

Family therapists suggest that a family will always try to restore its usual and familiar balance – a phenomenon known as homeostasis*. This tendency to adjust to the 'normal' way of being can result in pressure on one or more members of the family. This may be when a family calls on a social work agency, or their extended family for help (Burnham, 1986).

When noticing changes in the behaviour of your child(ren), it is useful to consider the events which may have changed your family structure.

Change can have an impact at all levels, or in any part of the family machine. For example, if a grandparent suddenly becomes ill and needs care, the attentions of the adults may be turned outside the immediate family and distracted from the effects on their children. Imagine that one of the siblings is particularly dominant or competitive, and normally kept in check by the adults. This is an opportunity for the child to become dominant. Thus, there are changes in family roles and relationships at a time when the adults in the family are pre-occupied with other events.

This can happen as a result of any major pressure or change, such as unemployment, illness, the breakdown of a relationship, or moving house and changing neighbourhood.

Your family structure

All family structures are different. Think about your family tree. It may help you to draw it. We have included examples of our own family trees to help you. Notice how different the structures look.

Key:

Male

Female

A cross through a square or circle means that that person has died.

Madan's Family Tree

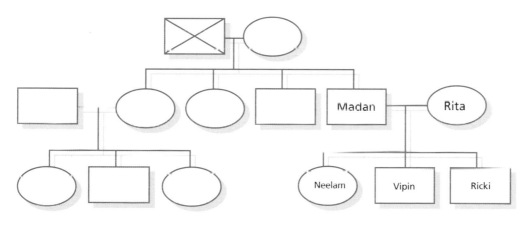

Berni's Family Tree

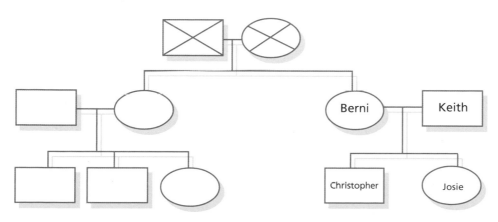

There are many events and experiences which punctuate family life and affect its relationships and dynamics. The impact of a life-changing event can ripple through your family for many years.

Activity

Identify your significant life events

Identify your significant life events from this list:

- ❏ births,
- ❏ starting school,
- ❏ illness,
- ❏ separations,
- ❏ hospitalisations,
- ❏ bereavements,
- ❏ moves,
- ❏ finances,
- ❏ leaving home,
- ❏ new partners.

You will recognise some of these and you will have some events of your own to add.

Take some time to think about these events. Identify the differences in your life – what was life like before your most significant event and what was life like after it?

Is there anyone significant that you need to share your thoughts with?

- Your partner?
- Your child?
- Your parents?
- A friend?

When you have had some time to think about this, you need to stand back from the events that you have identified. Consider the effects of these events on yourself, on others and on your relationships with them. Think of your family as a system, or a machine, dealing with the effect of an outside influence or a change in the usual functioning of one of its components.

Change may be immediately apparent, or it can dawn on you slowly, over time. It can be impactful, caused by circumstances within or outside your control. Change can affect any part of the 'system' or family member or the whole of the family system.

If you go to a counsellor, or seek outside help for your concerns, then part of the assessment they make may be about your history. It may also include significant events in your life that have resulted in difference or change.

Analysing famous families!

Think of a family with whom you are familiar. You may know the family well, or you could choose a fictional family – one from a TV show or a soap opera.

Consider the history of this family in relation to these questions:

- What are the significant events in the life of this family?
- Who has moved in and out of the family?
- What happens when there is a birth, a marriage, a divorce, a death, or a separation caused by other circumstances?
- What has been the effect of changing finances or environments on the family?

When you have thought through the history of the family, choose one or two individual family members.

Consider how these people have changed in response to life events.

- Do you think that the change happened instantly, over time, or with maturity?
- In what way did they change?
- Did they become stronger, weaker, caring, loving, distant, relaxed or hostile?
- What were the effects of these changes on other family members?
- ow did the family develop in response to this?

Families tend to maintain their routines so that change evolves slowly over time. Some family systems adapt well to change. A good example of this is a family system evolving and changing to accommodate the needs of children growing up and reaching adolescence. If an event occurs to interfere with this process, or set it off course, then difficulties can arise. Thus, it is helpful to be aware that whilst change and difference are for the most part healthy and useful, it can sometimes be difficult for each family member (component or cog) to adapt in a way that is most helpful to the system.

Family belief systems

As families, and the individuals within them, adapt and evolve over time, relationships change too. However, it is not only relationships that change – what you believe about yourself and the other members of your family circle can also alter.

Families generate stories about their members that can be passed down through generations, creating and reinforcing 'belief systems' about particular events.

This is how families know and come to understand their world. As a new member joining a family, for example as an in-law, or an adopted or fostered child, some of the unwritten rules, legends and assumptions understood by the other members can escape you.

The family's ability to create 'family scripts' is a well-known idea suggested by Byng Hall in 1984. Family scripts are established stories that travel down through generations and are 'transmitted' through the language used in families. These are the 'catch phrases', special words or 'mottos' that are unique to your family. Some are easy to recognise because they are heard often, for example 'father is always right', 'a house without children is an empty house', and 'the women in this family live longest'.

Over time, families come to believe that these catch phrases are true, even if they have no basis in fact or actual events. Sometimes the language or phrases can fall away and the 'ideas' remain. Family members subscribe to the ideas, but do not know why. These then become *belief systems*.

Your family's belief systems

You might like to discuss these with your partner, or compare them to the belief systems of friends' families.

In addition, each culture has its own unique and recognised set of traditions and beliefs. These inform a family's understanding about a range of important events, such as childcare, marriage, the care of elders, and the position of sons and daughters in a family (this was referred to in the 'Children of Six Cultures' study in part 1).

Review

This section is an important one, but you may have found it difficult to work through because some of the information is new, and may not easily fit into your schema about families.

If you did find it difficult, don't worry! Work through it again, at your own pace, and use your own experiences as a guide. Focus on what is useful to you. You may wish to discuss what you have found helpful in this section with your partner, or a member of your group.

Try to keep a note of your thoughts so that you can look back over them in the future, and track how your thinking has developed and moved forward. When you begin to reflect on your experiences, you begin to change the ideas you have had about them. In the next section we explore this further, and look at some more theory to illustrate how life events can affect your understanding, and ability to cope with change both emotionally and psychologically. That means how we think and how we feel about change, which in turn affects how we behave.

You will have lived in a family group all your life. Some people may have lived in children's homes, others in birth, foster or adoptive families. Change can affect long-term relationships in families. You may want to think about how your child's future family might be constructed. Imagine your family in the next five . . . ten . . . twenty . . . years.

Part Six

Learning from experiences

Learning from experiences

In the last section of this book you are going to consider another set of influential ideas – your own. You will be able to use your own personal belief systems to deal with issues or problems that arise in your life.

happy	angry
pleased	cross
excited	guilty
grateful	enraged
content	worried

Personal construct psychology

The 'personal construct psychology' theories of George Kelly, an American psychologist, were first published in 1955. They were developed as a way of explaining how an individual makes sense of his/her life experiences and beliefs.

Kelly was interested in why people behave as they do, and how they manage all the experiences they have in their daily life. He was curious about how people sort out their experiences, and what others could learn from people who effectively manage many different life events to help them overcome their own problems.

Kelly believed that people are the expert on their own learning and management of their own experiences.

Does this idea sound familiar to you?

He was interested in how this was tested out in day-to-day behaviour. Feelings associated with a particular type of behaviour are given a name, e.g. happy, sad or angry. These are named even though they describe a personal experience or *feeling* and are not *real*, you can't for example hold *sad* in your hand.

Over time everybody develops ideas about how certain experiences make them feel, and these ideas are called constructs*. Every construct you have developed is a theory to help you make reasonable predictions about your life, and communicate your expectations about it to others.

People begin to develop constructs with their very first experience being dependent on parents or carers for food and warmth. If this is satisfied, we build a construct or theory that associates our carer with providing for and soothing us. This feeling could be called 'contentment' or 'satisfaction'.

Can you think of any other words to describe it?

Constructs are built from individual experiences, and therefore the same experience will mean different things to different people. The words you use to describe your experience of the world may mean something different to someone else. A good example of this are the words 'solid' and 'cool' which mean something different to your teenager than to you!

By remembering past experiences, people make guesses about new situations. (Remember the example of the dog?) They may decide to check out their hunches, or decide not to continue the relationship or interaction further.

Activity

Applying the theory to an example

Think about these examples:

1) A woman has been subjected to domestic violence for many years at the hands of her male partner.

   She knows that when he becomes loud this means he is getting angry, and when he is angry he hits her. Thus, she becomes fearful when he becomes loud.

   Her construct is that *loud* means aggressive behaviour and physical hurt.

   She might carry this idea into other situations. So when her son, new partner or neighbour becomes overly loud, she overreacts to avoid harm or protect herself. As a result she puts herself in conflict with others.

   This example shows that your past experiences can influence how you think, feel and express yourself in the face of each new experience you have. The construct of *loud* or *angry* will be different for the woman in the example above than for others who have not been hurt or frightened by someone else's anger.

   Your personal construct of each of your experiences creeps into and influences day-to-day relationships. It can influence them for better or worse.

   This is represented in the diagram below.

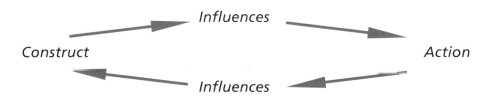

Influences

Construct   Action

Influences

To follow our example through:

When her son's behaviour becomes loud, the woman overreacts. Her son then gets increasingly annoyed and shouts louder at her.

She either becomes more fearful and gives in, or more determined and forceful in her attempts to control him.

Either way, the outcome is not favourable for mother or son because the personal constructs she has learnt in one relationship have been transferred to another.

- Do you think it would be different if the mother understood her son's construct of this situation, i.e. what was influencing his behaviour?

- What constructs might the child develop over time if these experiences are repeated?

- How does your children's understanding of the world affect you, and how does yours affect them?

- Consider how children make sense of the world, how their vocabulary develops, and how it can shape and inform their understanding.

- Remember that children learn from what they see happening around them. As a parent or carer you are a powerful role model, but so, also, are their friends.

- Consider the influence of the media in informing constructs about the world.

2) Consider the example below of a disagreement between a mother and daughter. Suppose the daughter has arrived home late from a party:

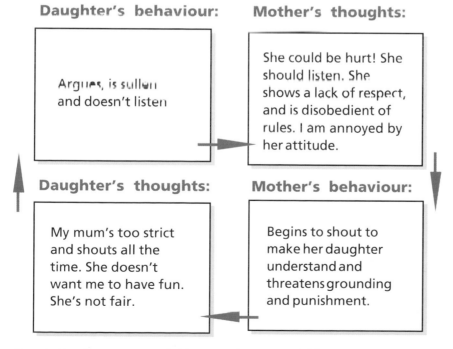

Daughter's behaviour:

Argues, is sullen and doesn't listen

Mother's thoughts:

She could be hurt! She should listen. She shows a lack of respect, and is disobedient of rules. I am annoyed by her attitude.

Daughter's thoughts:

My mum's too strict and shouts all the time. She doesn't want me to have fun. She's not fair.

Mother's behaviour:

Begins to shout to make her daughter understand and threatens grounding and punishment.

Track the boxes round. Try starting at a different box each time and see if your own construct about blame changes. In this example, a miscommunication has occurred and, if not resolved, could interfere in future relationships, hurting both mother and daughter.

Activity

Applying the theory at home

Can you think of any examples of miscommunication in your relationship with your own child(ren)? It is a good idea to use a real example. If your children are old enough you could try doing it with them. If you do this start each sentence with "I feel . . .".

Fill in the boxes below with your example.

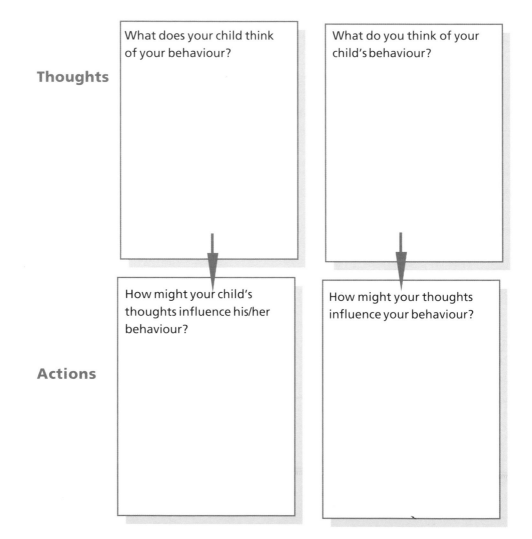

Thoughts

What does your child think of your behaviour?

What do you think of your child's behaviour?

Actions

How might your child's thoughts influence his/her behaviour?

How might your thoughts influence your behaviour?

This activity is about how people influence each other's thoughts, feelings and behaviour. Being aware of how your experiences have influenced your thoughts and feelings and consequently your behaviour, can help you to interact more effectively with those around you, and, more importantly, with your children.

However, you can change your own personal constructs – you can influence how your experiences cause you to think and feel. Being responsive to your experiences in a way which is helpful to you can increase your emotional and psychological *resilience**.

The importance of resilience

To be resilient is to adapt and change in a way that maintains your emotional and psychological wellbeing, particularly when faced with situations that are threatening or cause anxiety in day-to-day life.

You have learnt that early life experiences affect your resilience and ability to cope, and ongoing life experiences continually add to your knowledge. An understanding of how you have arrived at the present, and the influence of relationships on your wellbeing, can increase your capacity to cope.

Although stress and trauma can be disabling when they occur, the understanding and experience of coping with them leads to personal growth and resilience. Learning this about yourself can enable you to nurture those skills in your children as they develop self-esteem and self-identity.

George Kelly (1955) developed the idea that there are five stages through which individuals develop constructs. He called these five stages the 'experience cycle'. The experience cycle consists of:

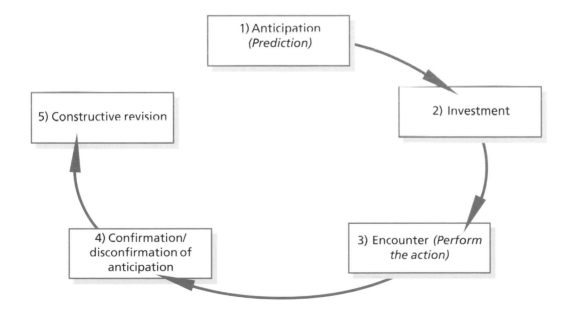

Individuals can develop resilience through the same process.

Think about

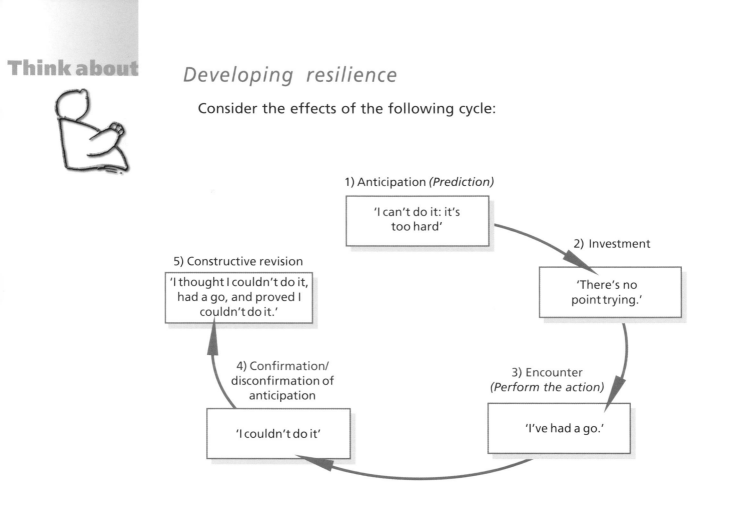

Developing resilience

Consider the effects of the following cycle:

1) Anticipation *(Prediction)*

'I can't do it: it's too hard'

2) Investment

'There's no point trying.'

5) Constructive revision

'I thought I couldn't do it, had a go, and proved I couldn't do it.'

4) Confirmation/ disconfirmation of anticipation

'I couldn't do it'

3) Encounter *(Perform the action)*

'I've had a go.'

From step one to step five of this cycle, the message is a negative one. The person continually repeating this pattern of thoughts and experience will learn it as a construct. They are not resilient enough (for many reasons which may be beyond their control) to challenge those things that are problematic to them. They have learnt a personal message about ability, success and challenge Significant people in their life could have encouraged them to internalise this message.

To increase confidence and self-esteem, the self-taught message needs to be changed, and the cycle of negative thinking interrupted. A construct can be an emotional feeling as well as a verbal message or set of thoughts.

Think about

The following diagram illustrates how constructs can be changed.

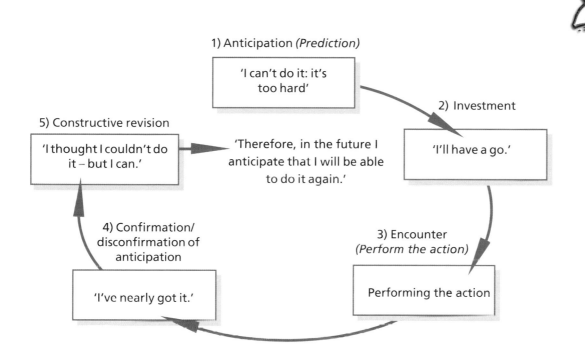

1) Anticipation *(Prediction)*
'I can't do it: it's too hard'

2) Investment
'I'll have a go.'

3) Encounter *(Perform the action)*
Performing the action

4) Confirmation/ disconfirmation of anticipation
'I've nearly got it.'

5) Constructive revision
'I thought I couldn't do it – but I can.'

'Therefore, in the future I anticipate that I will be able to do it again.'

Success has not been achieved in either example. However, the difference between the two is the 'sense' that is made of the experience. The first is a negative experience that could influence the person's efforts in the future; the second a positive experience they can learn from.

The ability to talk to yourself in a positive way (positive self-talk*), and the ability to turn a negative experience into a positive one, is a powerful way of coping with difficult times, surviving intact, and increasing your resilience. It is the skill of finding the silver lining in a cloud, or believing that a glass is half-full, not half-empty. People experience similar events in a different way. Part of dealing with traumatic and difficult experiences is to be able to use them to learn new things about yourself.

Think about

Your successes

- Think of someone you admire or look up to. Perhaps you have been surprised in the past at their ability to stay calm under crisis, forgive a real hurt, or manage a very challenging situation. Think about what they learnt from that experience and how it could help them in the future.

- Identify past experiences when you did cope, achieved something, or found a personal, inner strength that you didn't know you had.

The skill of telling yourself "I have survived" increases your resilience. You can help yourself develop resilience, and prepare yourself for a challenge, by positive self-talk.

Negative self-talk simply destroys the effects of your positive self-talk – your resilience, self-esteem and confidence. Language influences thoughts, which influence behaviour and emotions. (Sapir-Wharf, 1947).

Nervous actors and entertainers give themselves a positive self-talk before a performance. A football coach does the same for his/her players. Remember that what you say and do has an effect on you and those around you, particularly your children. Do you remember discussing your own views and attitudes on children and society in part one? It is not possible to change *how* you absorbed these messages, but it is possible to change *what* you do with them in the future.

As a parent or carer your task is twofold: to develop your own coping abilities and to develop the coping abilities and resilience of your children. The next time you feel yourself getting angry or wound-up with your children, try giving yourself a *calming* self-talk. Work out your script in advance though. Think of some calming messages now, and practise them. You might want to compare your messages with your partner's, or discuss them with a friend.

Remember, the best time to practise is before the event!

Conclusion

The final sections of this book have focused on the structure of family groups, and shown you how the most significant people in your life influence your ability to cope, and develop and increase your self-esteem.

We hope that this last chapter has enabled you to bring together the experiences you have remembered with everything you have learnt whilst working through this book. We hope you have begun to understand how your personal constructs have evolved over a lifetime and influenced you in the present. You have the potential to influence your children and provide for them satisfying experiences of attachment, nurturing, stimulation and play and, above all, of being listened to and valued.

Finally, think about what you have learnt from this book. What will you take with you?

Consider which parts have been the most and the least useful parts. If you have kept a journal, this is probably a good time to review it and decide if you will share it with anyone – your own parents? Your partner? Your children?

We hope that you will have discovered new things and confirmed established ideas.

Your future development is influenced by experience and feedback – and so is ours! We welcome feedback and comments to influence our future work. You can contact us via the publisher: we will reply to you and will be glad to receive your views.

Glossary

Use this to look up words that are unfamiliar to you. The definitions given here relate to how the words are used in this text.

Attachment: A close emotional bond felt by one person towards another.

Aural: Related to the sense of hearing.

Barometer: An instrument to measure atmospheric pressure, used here as a metaphor to illustrate an example.

Behaviour modification: A method of teaching people to change their behaviour by the systematic use of reinforcements.

Biologically: Regarding biology – a study of living organisms, such as plants, animals or humans.

Bonding: Forming a bond, or a close attachment, or affiliation, between individuals and groups.

Conditional: Dependent on something else.

Construct: To build, or put together, a set of thoughts or ideas.

Culture: Often related to heritage, the customs, ideas, art, etc. that influences the way in which people in a group, society, or nation interact.

Ego: The part of the personality that helps you to deal with the external world and its demands, and the effect of your own needs.

Emotional glue: The feelings that 'stick' people together.

Genes: The basic unit of genetic material, which pre-determines parts of our appearance and personality.

Genetically: Determined by our genes.

Homeostasis: The tendency to keep things the same.

Impactful: Any event or experience which leaves an impression on you.

Interaction: The influence of two or more people or things on each other.

Internalised: To become part of one's personality.

Maturation: The process of development to maturity.

Metaphor: A comparison made to illustrate an example or story.

Modalities: A word used to describe the medium or sense through which an event is experienced.

Olfactory: Relating to the sense of smell.

Oral: Spoken or verbal.

Positive self talk: To talk or think to yourself, emphasising the good in an experience.

Psychodynamic theory: To consider the effects of early life experiences on present beliefs and behaviour.

Psychotherapeutic: To be involved in a relationship or activity that helps one to understand the effect of life experiences on feelings and emotions.

Resilience: The ability to bounce back or cope with something.

Schema: A mental framework or set of ideas that are based on your own experience.

Siblings: Brothers and sisters.

Socialisation: The means by which people learn the social rules that a community lives by.

Stimulus: Something that has an impact on something else, moving it to action.

System: A sequence of events or set of parts which, although separate, can function together. Applied to family therapy or group therapy.

Bibliography

Alladin, W. *Models of Counselling and Psychotherapy for a Multiethnic Society, in* Palmer and Laungani (1999) *op. cit.*

Allen, N. (1992) *Making Sense of the Children Act,* Longman.

Atkinson, R.C. and Shiffrin (1968) 'Human memory: a proposed system and its control process', in Cohen, Kiss and Levoi (1977), Open University Press.

Baddeley, A.D. and Hitch, G. (1974) *Working Memory* in Cohen, Kiss and Le Voi, *Memory, Current Issues* (1993) Open University Press.

Baddeley, et al (1981) *Psychology an Integrated Approach,* Eysenck, M. (ed) (1998) Longman.

Bandura, A. (1977) *Social Learning Theory,* Englewood Cliffs and Prentice Hall.

Batchelor, J., Dimmock, B. and Smith, D. (1994) *Understanding Stepfamilies,* Stepfamily Books.

Berne, E. (1964) *Games People Play,* Grove Press.

Bowlby, J. (1975) *Separation, Anxiety and Anger,* Pelican, Harmondsworth.

Brown, A.L. and Deloache, J.S. (1983) *Metacognitive Skills,* in Donaldson, M. (ed) *Early Childhood Development and Education,* Blackwell.

Brown, G. and Harris, T. (1978) *The Social Origins of Depression,* Tavistock.

Burnham, J. (1991) *Family Therapy,* Routledge.

Burr, V. (2000) *An Introduction to Social Constructionism,* Routledge.

Cohen, G. et al (1997) *Memory: Current Issues,* Open University Press.

Colman, A.M. (2001) *Dictionary of Psychology,* Oxford University Press.

De'ath, E. and Slater, D. (1992) *Parenting Threads,* Step Family Publications, The National Step Family Association.

Furman, B. (1999) *It's Never Too Late to Have a Happy Childhood,* BT Press.

Goldenson, R.M. (1984) *Longman Dictionary of Psychology and Psychiatry,* Longman.

Hall, B. (1984) in Burnham, J. (1991) *op. cit.*

Harper, L. and Huie, K. (1985) in Wood (1995) *Basic Psychology,* Hodder and Stoughton.

Hetherington and Parkes (1993) *Child Psychology: A Contemporary Viewpoint,* 3rd Edition, McGraw Hill.

Holmes, T. and Rahe, R. (1967) *The Social Readjustment Scale,* Journal of Psychosomatic Research No.11 pp. 213–218.

Kelly, G. (1955) *The Psychology of Personal Constructs,* Vols. 1 & 2, W. W. Norton.

Locke, J. (1632–1704) cited in Oates, J. (1994) *The Foundations of Child Development,* Blackwell.

McMahon, L. (1992) *The Handbook of Play Therapy,* Routledge.

Mead, G.H (1934) *Mind, Self, and Society,* University of Chicago Press.

Metcalf, L. in Ben Furman (1999) *op. cit.*

Me Varech, Z., Silber, O. and Fine, D. (1991) *Learning with computers in small groups: cognitive and affective outcomes,* Journal of Computing Research, 7(2).

Miell, D. and Dallas, R. (1996) *Social Interaction & Personal Relationships,* Sage Publications.

Oates, J. (1994) *The Foundations of Child Development,* Blackwell Publishers Ltd.

Palmer, S. and Luangani, P. (1999) *Counselling in a Multicultural Society,* Sage.

Reber, A.S. (1995) *Dictionary of Psychology,* 2nd edition, Penguin Books Ltd.

Rousseau, J. (1712–1778) cited in Oates, J. (1994) *op. cit.*

Sapir, E. (1947) *Selected Writings in Language, Culture and Personality,* in Burr (2000) *op. cit.*

Schwarz, J. (1999) *Cassandra's Daughter: A History of Pychoanalysis in Europe and America,* Penguin Press.

Thomas, M. and Pierson, J. (1995) *Dictionary of Social Work,* Collins Educational.

Thompson and Rudolph (1999) *Counselling Children,* 5th edition, Brooks/Cole.

Trevarthen (1992) *The function of emotions in early infant communication and development,* in Nadel, J. and Camioni, L. (eds) *New Perspectives in Early Development,* Routledge.

Vygotsky, L. (1933) *Play and its role in the mental development of the child,* in Damon, W. (1983) *Social and Personality Development,* W.W. Norton.

Vygotsky, L. (1962) *Thought and Language,* in Lee and Gupta (1995) *Children's Cognitive and Language Development,* Blackwell Publishers Ltd.

Whiting, B.B. and Whiting, J.W.M. (1975) *Children of Six Cultures: A Psycho-cultural Analysis,* Harvard University Press, cited in Oates, J. (1994).

Wilkinson, J. and Campbell, E. (1997) *Psychology in Counselling and Therapeutic Practice,* Wiley.

Winnicott, D.W. (1990) *Maturational Processes and the Facilitating Environment,* Karnac Publishing.

Winnicott, D.W. (1963) *Childcare and the Psychoanalytic Environment,* in Winnicott (1990) *op. cit.*